Tangled by Blood

Tangled by Blood

a memoir in verse
by Rebecca Evans

MOON
TIDE PRESS

~ 2023 ~

Tangled by Blood

Editor-in-chief
Eric Morago

Editor Emeritus
Michael Miller

Copy Editor
Betty Rodgers

Marketing Specialist
Ellen Webre

Proofreader
LeAnne Hunt

Cover and interior art
Amber Helton

Author photo
Taylor Badzic

Book design
Michael Wada

Moon Tide logo design
Abraham Gomez

Tangled by Blood
is published by Moon Tide Press

Moon Tide Press
6709 Washington Ave. #9297
Whittier, CA 90608
www.moontidepress.com

FIRST EDITION

Printed in the United States of America

ISBN #978-1-957799-08-7

Further Praise for *Tangled by Blood*

With *Tangled by Blood*, Rebecca Evans gives witness to a journey through pain and trauma and broken-ness, detailing the cyclic patterns of familial abuse while moving, poem by poem, in the direction of words like *joy* and *love*. Evans offers a clear-eyed and unflinching vision of what it means to become a survivor with poems that are "something like chanting, / something like prayer." By the book's end, the cycle of violence and abuse is broken, and *Tangled by Blood* delivers us to a new and ancient place—where poetry serves as a form of medicine.

— Brian Turner, author of *Here, Bullet* and *The Wild Delight of Wild Things*

Tangled by Blood, Rebecca Evans's riveting memoir in verse, is a delicate balance of poetic beauty and brutal memories. Evans's willingness to explore these instances of abuse through the perspective of perpetrators and prey, both, gives the collection a foundation of clear-eyed reflection that lifts this story up out of its murky depths to something brighter, something akin to hope.

— Patricia Ann McNair, author of *Responsible Adults*

Tangled by Blood asks the reader to imagine what many would deem unimaginable: a girl of five and her older sister endure sexual assaults by a father, and the devastating enabling, silence, and blame of a mother. The poems weave visceral and disturbing violence with images and language so beautiful that the juxtaposition is both startling and grounding. Through a wide range of emotional and tonal energies, Evans' generosity creates space for both sisters and the mother to speak, to tell their own stories, and each is treated with a stunning tenderness that extends to the reader as we are asked to bear witness with the speakers. Poems that forefront the mother's voice are simultaneously the most difficult and admirable: they present a woman distorted by her own abused past, resigned to an abusive present, and then allows and enables her own daughters' abuse. Evans tells us this collection is "an offering of what my body has done in the world, / what I've done with my body, what has been done to my body." It also offers a story of survival; of a refusal to allow the cycle of violence to spiral into the next generation; and, finally, a hard-won rebirth into the world, one populated with fruit trees grown from discarded seeds; fragrant, nourishing drinks; a weighted blanket; her three sons, loved and safe; a hot tub under the stars. Evans reimagines the unimaginable in these searing and necessary poems.

— Maggie Queeney, Stanley Kunitz Memorial Prize winner, and author of *In Kind*

Tangled by Blood explores mother/lack of mothering/bad mothering and finally asks the question: how does one learn to mother when she herself has been poorly mothered? Through lyricism, shifting viewpoints, and wordplay, these poems explore childhood trauma and the resulting fractured identity and selfhood, but also what it takes to break silences in order to make oneself whole, and finally how to mother the self. It's a brave and beautiful book.

— Suzanne Roberts, author of *Animal Bodies: On Death, Desire,*
and Other Difficulties

In Rebecca Evans' memoir, *Tangled by Blood,* she attempts to control the horrors of her childhood and the long-term effects of sexual trauma within the confines of the poetic form. The memoir consists of three sections and does not follow a linear narrative arc, but instead flows back and forth through the events of her life using different voices, perspectives, and forms. And "While the memoir moves into the joy and redemption she finds from motherhood, it is a powerful and difficult piece to read. Yet, the work is beautiful in the way it defies traditional narrative form and allows Evans to tell her story of survival on her terms.

— J. Reagon, book reviewer from *Memoir Magazine*

In fierce and unrelenting honesty, Rebecca Evans' poems and prose poems explore the memory of the body, of her family's dysfunction, her step-father's abuse, her mother's denial, and her sister's delicate protectiveness. It is a powerful exploration of the scars she and her sister carry, and of how resilience, even when it comes, carries its own price. In these unflinching pieces, readers will discover the poet's deeper story as well as a courageous discipline, the deep practice of entering hard experience through a brave art of speaking out. These poems are skilled songs speaking to the mother, of the Mother, and finally of the transformation to becoming a better mother. These will move you in both their skill and their heart.

— Anne-Marie Oomen, author of *As Long as I Know You*

Contents

NOTE: *TW Content – childhood sexual trauma, domestic violence, suicide*

for my sisters

I wanted to be your womb
(Tina)

Do you remember
when we were young,
bathing in bubbles,
water lapping our legs,
our skinned knees
kissing as we faced
each other, as we faced
sky with our bruised

petals? Baby Sister,
I tried to stay
brave as Daddy
entered, "helping" me
wash. You'd stay
still, stay quiet and unblinking
as he reached between
my thighs, his fingers

disappearing.

My tears splattered,
our shared ocean.
Sometimes, I'd say, "That hurts,"
And you pressed
your scabbed knees
into me, like tiny fire-

fly caresses. Later,
you'd say you wished
for his attention first,
you'd wonder why
you were chosen last.

I couldn't tell you,
Beckala, "He saves the best
for later," I wouldn't say,
"He doesn't know

what he's missing."
I only wanted you not
to want him. Only wanted you
to soak alone in our sacred
wound, knowing I offered
my flesh for his rejection of you.

Arithmetic

I spelled.

When I entered kindergarten, I didn't know my last name started with "A." Didn't know, because of that "A," I should sit first seat, first row. Didn't understand the ordering of letters. I'd not heard the alphabet. I'd not heard my last name. I didn't know my last name.

I spelled arithmetic.

My adopted sister, Tina, five years older, taught me counting. I counted to ten. She used my toes, wiggled them, giggling me silly. So, even though I didn't know my letters, I knew my numbers, but only one through ten. I also knew "This Little Piggy" and how to wee, wee, wee all the way home.

I spelled arithmetic in fourth grade.

In fourth grade, they diagnosed me with bleeding ulcers. At recess, my teacher stayed inside, shared her lunch—peanut butter and jelly—creamy and smooth and spread on the softest, whitest bread. We crafted cards for relatives I'd invented. She told me, "You're smart," though, at the time, I fake-read and gathered stories from ear and heart. I pretended. I pretended well.

I spelled arithmetic in a spelling bee while in the fourth grade.

When I won the spelling bee, spelling arithmetic, I couldn't tell my teacher the way I'd memorized the words on the list. I wanted her to think me smart, believe me something else, someone else. I'd memorized the list by forming sentences of each word. A Red Indian Thought He Might Eat Taffy In Church. I apologize now for my limited Native-American lens. At the time, I was nine. This was 1976. I didn't know better. I didn't know much.

I won the school spelling bee when I was in fourth grade.

I beat the entire school, even the sixth graders. My teacher treated me out to lunch. I forged Mother's signature on the permission slip. I knew forging because I witnessed Mother forging Aunt Glady's checks. At lunch, I ordered bacon. Ordered a BLT with extra bacon. Ordered fries and coleslaw too. I ate slow because I wanted lunch to linger. I wanted to live with my teacher. I wanted her to adopt me and, together, we could create cards for real relatives.

When I won the spelling bee, they gave me a Snoopy trophy.

Mother tossed the trophy in the trash.

Mother wasn't mad about my winning. She wasn't mad about my forging. She wasn't mad I'd earned a reward. She wasn't mad I'd eaten bacon. She was mad that I "lied" to the doctor when he found my bleeding ulcers. She was mad I answered, "Daddy," when the doctor asked, "Who damaged you?" If I couldn't live with my teacher, I'd choose to stay at the hospital. I'd pray for cancer, something deadly, something to guide me, help me wee, wee, wee all the way home.

I dug the trophy from the trash, hid it in my sock drawer, towards the back.

You do the math.

I spelled arithmetic.

Mother warned me that pork would burn my blood. What she meant was we were Jewish and her husband, my stepfather, was a deacon and we pretend-lived un-Jewish-like. She warned me young while she fried bacon in our kitchen, "This will turn you bad." At my reward-lunch with my teacher, I ate bacon, believing myself already bad. How much bad can one person be?

I let the salt sit on my tongue. I hoped my blood would boil—black, blue, red—burst to flame.

I spelled.

Later, when Daddy called me, "Stupid," again, I knew better. I knew my letters now. I knew my last name too. I knew how to spell, and I knew I'd learn to read. I knew he lied and Mother lied and I understood lying. I understood our house, built on lies, forced me to pretend-dumb just to survive. I pretended. I pretended well. I pretended so well that I believed this lie. I believed this lie until I lost myself. I lost myself until I found myself. I found myself following words down the page, penning them through sound and heart. I turned lines into math and music. I sang wee, wee, wee all the way home.

Arithmetic.

Toothless

(Beckala)

You're OK, Mommy. Whatever
Daddy did, he didn't mean
it. The dentist? The dentist
took your teeth? How can you
eat, Mommy? Mom?
I'll take care of you.
I promise. Yes. You look
so pretty. Just as pretty
as before. No. No one
will notice. Even without
your teeth. You want me
to change? Wear black?
Cover my mouth? Oh.
Cover it when I smile.

Pretending to Swallow

Mother.

I kept clothed, Garanimals: plum-hued hippos,
like a bulged bruise, my delicate white
socks ruffling my ankles. Where was Mother
when he slipped my panties aside, exposed
me and, then, exposed
himself?

Mother was.

I'd leave my room legless, grip the entry-
frame, stand straight, stand *fine*.
You better not start that crying and I didn't.
I did not. Even today, I still
have not. I've not cried over the death
of my purity.

Mother was worse.

Violence: silent as unheard prayer
fraying indigo-inked sky.
Sometimes waves rush my mind,
drowning Daddy's grunts,
my body suffering his final thrust.

Mother was worse than.

At least Mother didn't restrain me
while he rode. She remained one room
away, watching *Hollywood Squares,*
or further, at the counter, shoving shredded
beef and onions into gaping green peppers,
christening each with tomato sauce.

Mother was worse than Father.

At dinner, I'd spread my food, pretend-
eat, spoon portions in my napkin
stretched cross my thighs, seeming
to swallow,
to swig,
to swill,
as Mother leaned near,

Such a big appetite.

Talking About Me in Front of Me

(Mother)

She's such a big
will. Too much for her own
good. Really. She's fine.
Just look how she bites
her nails. To the core. See?
Nervous Little Twit.
Her twitches. One
of many. Now, Becky, tell
the nice doctor the real
story. You need to tell
the truth. She invents
these fantasies.
Her way, her way to gather
attention. See? Like this
hospital stay. Honestly. I'm
sure she's "doing it" already.
With schoolboys. I know. Yes.
Yes, she's old enough.
She's nine.

Hebetic Interludes in Middle School Changing Rooms

I clutched my clothes behind gym
lockers, unlatched my bra
beneath two slack shirts, slipping
my arms in and out of sleeves—
sleight of hand, out of sight—

as if I were witch, magician. Other
days, I bunched my pants
and tanks, sealed myself in a stall.
Like the lovely box jumper—
wave of wand—*poof*—disappear.

The others wore their pubic fluff,
cupped baby breasts and compared,
Look at your bush, girl,
and, *At least you have hair.*
and, *Have you had your*
monthly visitor? and *How long*

do you bleed? I kept my lips
tight, feared I'd blurt, *I'd been*
bleeding since I was four or five.
(Just not that way.) My decay
stayed, whirling within,
yearning to shed.

A Soft Food Diet Doesn't Always Heal the Heart

Mother's brittle stones, rotted
from the inside. Her gums
blackened, decaying roots
as she learned to live
on Jello and mashed KFC
and things she could swallow

whole. Later, she'd place her fake grin
in cloudy Polident waters. Her smile
reached half-way and only on the right
side. When I saw it, I knew best
to maintain quiet, bleed worry into my belly.

I can't remember her voice, if she laughed
out loud or at all, but I do know, even
now, the smell of her breath, hot, like
tar, like something within her seared.

If I unclench my teeth, I'll scream, afraid
I won't stop, rattling my insides,
quaking my memory of Mother
watching Daddy shake on top of me,
hollowing me into numbness
only the decayed can understand.

Of Birth and Blessings

Blessed are you, child of Divine, of destruction. If
unblessed, you, daughter risen from nothing. From no-one I
blessed. Are you scraping vernix from your tongue? Unclench.
Unbless your mother, once a fetus, once My yellowed teeth.

Blessed, are you not formed from her bone and biofilm? I'll
unbless your host in her postnatal weeks. Scream
blessings. Are you squalling? Squawk in a silent way, afraid.
Unbless your taken body—take back your womb, for I

blessed. Are you crying celestial tears? You won't
unbless your men. You invite them in to dine. You stop
blessed pain with tourniquets 'round your neck, rattling
unblessings. You siren through pinched lips and fractured breath. My

Blessed, Are you my child formed from tissue of unprotected insides?
Unblessed you. Hip-thrusting Hurricane. You. Waking and quaking
blessings. Are you spooning out your eyes? Unseeing My
unblessings. You tired? Yet? Child-birth through labored memory-

blessings. Are you sure you long to perish, a death woven only of
unblessings. You blame Me. Blame Banshees. Blame Mother.
Blessed are you, the silent-keeper, the lip-sealer—watching
unblessedness. You look for *him* in every man. Daddy.

Blessed are you, child of all things holy—an apple, a snake. Shake
unblessings you ring forth like bells: holding cathedrals, holding on.
Blessed are you, bleeding daughter, belly-swelled beneath top(s).
Unbless you. Sneeze the devil from your labia lips, your scars of

blessedness. Are you coming? Are you leaving? Are you having fun with Me
unblessing you? You give in to shallowing, cowering, your fire-hollowing.
Blessed are you, woman-wolf howling at sky. At moon. At Me.
Unbless your hunger. Starve into wonder and wake one morning into

Blessedness. Are you feeling anything? Are you numb to your numbness?
Unbless you who knows who to curse, cuss, and circumcise. The only
Blessed. Are you crazy from your cravings? Are you speaking in tongues? The
unblessed You with your skirt smoothed slick. Your hair coifed, decayed (&)

blessed. Are you a child of the God on High? On Low? Can
unblessings save you? You. Blessed and Unblessed, now know. Now understand.

Echoes of Lunch

(Mother)

If you were skipping
lunch, you should
have given it back.
Yes.
I took it.
It was mine.

Shoes?
You need to buy new shoes?
You think I'm jealous?
Of track spikes? Your Keds?
Your constant need of attention?

Look at my feet.
Get on the ground.
See how they hang over?
Not because I'm fat.
They're swollen.
Try being a waitress.

And, Becky, what do you do?
Jump around in a short skirt?
Run in circles?
You think I don't know your age?
You think I care you're 13.

All you care about is your tiny, tanned body.
You won't stay small. Just wait.
You run track to show off
your legs in tight shorts. You think
you're better than me? You think
you're special? You think
anyone cares you won a race? You think
anyone cares? What are you

crying for? Don't look at me like that.

Cremation

Some days, his salty
sweat strikes me between
the eyes and I blink his shadow
from on top of me,
push his weight

to the side and find
I'm flinching—at the wheel,
beneath bed covers,
kneeling on stone
shower floors.

If he asks forgiveness
for my blood-streaked
panties, I'll wonder
if I'm capable,
when I'm incapable

of unremembering

Mother

blaming me, at 14,
for her husband's hunger—

as she curled
beside me
while he tore
their queen sheets,

stiff from the night before.

I try to un-see
her back flesh
folding over itself
as she turned
away, the wind carrying
her cherry scent,

silence following.

If she asks my forgiveness,
I'll fail her,
though we remain
tangled by blood.

When I'm asked
to honor Mother in death—
bear her ashes—I'll remind
them—Jews think *salach* a duty,
but we were also taught

war is often needed
to bring peace. I'd say,
Sinners crave repentance,
though Mother never said
Sorry, and I'll remind

them that Mother forgot
her origin.

Jews do not cremate the dead.

Honor Thy Mother

Honor thy Mother, though damaged and howling. Spew lava at last.
Honor thy Father in heaping ashes and trash. This hollowing year,
honor thyself, wife to none, mother to three, daughter of all. I

honor thy Mother's cocoon blanket of silk and skin. She once spilt,
Honor thy Father, thy son, thy holy ghosts—my shadow-self cursed that
honor. Thyself—my shedding transformation, singular meditation—one word:

honor. Thy Mother unprotected me, exposing belly and breast. Gods spit
dishonor of thy Father's abuse—I carried it, buried it, found my way and married
it. Honor thy self-inflicted wounds, unscab and bleed out, blend in. Scoff at

honoring thy Mother-rage—embrace drowning. Lose breath. Lose my
honor. Thy Father's stain remains, soiling lace, blemishing my reflection.
Honor. Thy. Self. Honor thy wealth of woe and unworth. Honor birth until

you honor thy Mother-hurt, then charter your daughter-self to slaughter. I
honor thy Father until haunted and hunted, the unwanted wanted. Punch
honoring thyself. And then rest—on back, on knees. Unleash my

honor from thy Mother's name. Hallowed—Pearl—oyster-grit imagining
honor. Thy Father's fist wasted on bone and bared back. Crushing. Busting
honor. Myself: thinning sheer, unwhispering prayer. Asking. *Where's my*

honor? Thy Mother carries pain like hummingbird nectar. She unfaced
honoring thy Father-need. The need to be heard, to be yearned, to
honor thyself-inflicted blistering. Burnished into whimpering. Crystalizing

honor. Thy Mother gave me away, sold my body to her devil-man, then
honored thy Father's touch. Mother's hands, unfed and hungry, balled,
Honor. Thyself. Now lost, myself given to the Father, tarnishing my

honor. Thy Mother, we wish her well. Wish her gone. Wish her fist-fulls
of dishonor. Thy father's breath holds wistful death, pushing
honorless love. Thyself, no longer self, no longer felt. Sit with it. Honor it.

Honor thy Mother's womb, her empty turned tomb, turned numb. To
honor thy Father's scent—sweat and soured milk—means holding my
honor. Thyself releasing burden and blame. Unseal your mouth.

Honor thy Mother of all things ancient and aching.
Honor thy Father's holy land, holy dwelling. To
honor thy Self, speak stars and light and stifle

dishonoring thy Mother. Smother hate and harm. The
honor of thy Fatherless life lies in another world, another word.
Honor thy Self. Plant poppies, grow grapes. Grow. I

honor thy Mother. She—no longer my disruption. Shout
honor at thy Father. He—no longer my extinction. It
honors thy Self to fill my womb with sons and hope, then

honor thy Mother for birthing me. Thankfulness whispered
in honor of thy Father. For I am me because of thee. It
honors thy Self to alchemy from death to life, turning

honor of my mother's path into lessons, into sun. That
I honor any father—with a father like mine—is proof, is word,
is honor of my Self. That I can honor my song shows: *This*

honor: my mother's reflection of me. Of all. Of words.
Honor the Father, so I might summit peaks, exit shadows. To
honor my Self means to honor all others and palm my pain into dust.

Relief

I was that girl slicing wrists in showers, certain
warm water-breath would rush life out. Uncertain
if I welcomed death or stormed alarms,
urging, *Someone find me* [alive]. Maybe I craved
a savior. Later, I'll date men striving to save

me. I was that girl swallowing pills, gulping
handfuls of aspirin [a pre-numbing for suffering
should I survive]. They pumped my belly
'til amber phlegm flowed. I stayed sad
[not gaining the good fortune to die].

I was that girl chocking chalky laxatives,
[ingesting entire boxes]. My insides cramped,
spilling fluids streaked with cardinal
blood. Skin thinned cross laced bones
[my body fuzzed with deprivation], disappearing

in bathrooms [to disappear]. I was that girl,
calloused first knuckle, harder heart, gouging,
purging until brown bile speckled
porcelain. I'd rinse [not swallow] until

tepid water turned sweet. I'm still the girl—
slicing and swallowing, gulping and gouging—
praying precious relief rinse away me-hating,
baptize and re-birth into girl [the girl, that girl],
still small, but *finally* [finally] at rest in her palm.

How to Cover a Bruise

Mother taught me to hide
facial bruising with concealer
and a tender touch.

> *First, tap on white,*
> *it covers purple,*
> *then, dab green*
> *to fade black.*

> *Don't rub. Pat. Avoid*
> *stretching skin. Don't*
> *encourage wrinkles*
> *at your age.*

I was 12.

She taught me food alleviates
hurt. Shovel it, in spoon-fulls
of mac and cheese. Slather
butter cross bread, bagels, and bulges.

> *Don't talk with your mouth*
> *full,* and, *if you stay*
> *full, you'll never feel hungry.*

She forgot to teach me to sit
with hunger, allowing vacancy
to spill into motivation.
She forgot to tell me, *Pain*
is a symptom of something wrong
instead of something to endure

or ignore.

Instead, she said, *Any man*
is better than no man, and
It's far worse to live
alone than face abuse.

(But facing yourself is worse.)

She taught me to suffer
prayer—cry in the shower
or the closet, muffled and muted—
don't return 'til the red
fades to yellow, then still blot
on more foundation, cover your mess.

> *Cover yourself, Young Lady.*

She once said that bare skin attracts
men and if I chose to expose my knees,
my collar bones, my panty lines,
I'd gather unwanted attention.

> *But any attention is better*
> *than no attention.*

I learned to paint a happy face
so I could stay damaged
in relationships.

Until I couldn't.

Later, I'll believe I've out-
grown her guidance. Believe
lifting my skirt might lift
my spirits. I'll tell myself,

> *Next time—*

because there's always a next
time—*I'll wear my bruising*
proud, something earned
instead of something to shroud.

At the Diner
(Mother)

Becky, you bring this on,
running 'round, hardly
clothed. Shorts. T-shirts.
What do you expect?
It's too tempting
for a man. Any real man.
You dress all sexy. Keep
your voice down, Young Lady.
Don't you make a scene
at my place of work.
Becky, you don't get it.
But you will.
You'll learn.
You'll learn
that any man is better
than no man.
You'll grow up.
You'll go on. And leave.
And guess what?
I'll still be here.
I'll be right here.

Talking to My First Boyfriend

(Beckalah — almost-Rebecca)

You'll be the first. Thank you
for going slow and waiting
these six coaxing months—
cocooning me before consuming me
in your stable shape. I know.

I'm still draped.

> *I can't.*
> *I can't explain why.*
> *It's not you.*
> *It's me.*

Thank you for stopping, kiss-
ing my lids. I know. I know
I'm not moving. I don't know
how. I don't think I can.

> *Go on.*
> *Go ahead.*
> *Just*
> *get it over with.*

I don't blame you for quitting,
quitting while on top of me.
Quitting on me. It's not you.
It's not me either. It's

> *Mother.*
> *Mother let bad things happen.*

Unspoken

As a girl, I didn't know the word.

When I'm four, or five, I'll learn
how secrets keep the word. Until
I learn—keeping secrets equals *bad*.

Miss Lewis teaches me about *Bad*—
good touch, bad touch. I'll strain
to grasp the difference. Once

I turn nine, my doctor treats my
ulcers, asks, *Who hurt you this way?*
And *Hurt* turns into the word.

Daddy,

I say. Mother shouts, *Liar!*
I believe her. Her word. Her
naming me. She calls this *Family*

Business. I hear, *Secret*. She warns,
Keep it to yourself and, *This is your
fault*. Gospel. When I marry, my

husband labels the word *Love*.
Tells me he feels it bigger, better.
Feels it all. Feels enough to lose

control. He echoes Mother's
It's your fault, adding, *No one
believes you* and *You're lucky.*

I trade *Luck* for *Love*. Then marry
Luck to *Bad*, knowing if I have any
luck at all, it's certainly bad.

Last year, I spilt that word, spit it
at my reflection, until I punched
my image, busting my face to crystals,

then balled my fist, pushed it into my
mouth, aching to stifle the word.
I shouted it. Then whispered it,

churning that word, this word, to dust.

The Confessional of Two or More

You never minded, but you mind and though
you hurt, you rarely hurt. You were used,
and, despite mindfulness, you use.

>   Never minded, you mind.
>   Hurt, you hurt rarely.
>   Used, you use.

Admit this. Your admission frees
the mind, offers permission, though
you won't permit more using.

>   Free admission
>   offers permission.
>   Admit. Using frees you.

They'll arrive—hurt you with your own
admission—until you realize you always
minded and all that mattered was their minding.

>   Admission hurts. They'll realize
>   you've arrived. All that mattered
>   is they admitted using you.
>   This. Admit.

Grown, and still, there's dusk-light bruising at daybreak

Before sun breaks sky, I'm criss-
crossed on my closet floor, my full-
                    [*Prepping*]
length reflecting. I once
claimed, *Painting my face.*
                    [*Hiding*]
The day before, my six-
year old bore witness,
                    [*I was wrong*]
watching me from the front
porch as his father held my wrist,
                    [*I get what I deserve*]
slamming car door cross
bone, cross flesh, four
                    [*Or maybe six*]
times. Open. Shut.
                    [*Open. Shut.*]
I whispered,
                    [*You're right*]
my lips shaping words
                    [*I was bad*]
before I could control
                    [*Please stop*]
their flow, my low moan.
                    [*It's my fault*]
My morning mirror reveals
                    [*Cover that shit*]
dusk-light bruising,
                    [*Cover yourself, Young Lady*]
yellows bleeding into plum,
                    [*It's fine*]
my arm angled, misshapen,
                    [*I'm fine*]
and my eyes, barely blue, barely there, hold
                    [*They once held oceans, held sky*]
nothing.

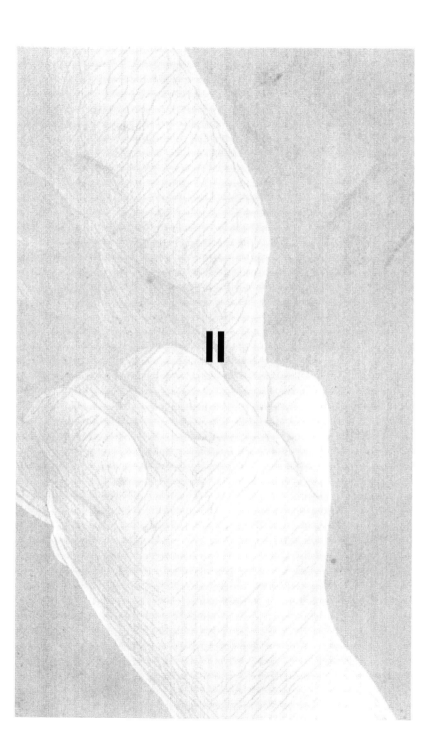

II

I wanted to be your wall
(*Tina*)

I

Do you remember
the early years
when I pushed my bed
between yours
and our bedroom door,

between Daddy and you,
night after night?
I was ten, maybe eleven.
He'd take me first,

while you laid
quiet in your twin,
listening to me
beg, "Please stop."
You'd still be next,

though I believed him
less angry if I bore
the brunt of his brutality.
Once he left, I'd pry
your fingers from your

blanket, pull our beds
together, both of us still
smelling of Old Spice
and his spoiled-milk-
breath. I curled you

like a mother would,
smoothing wet bangs
from your face. I did
it for you, Beckala. You
were only five and I knew
our hearts, our bodies,
were irreparable.

II

Do you remember
when I first became
your big sister,
a ward straight
from the state,
my body pocked
with cigarette burns

and you asked why
someone thought
me an ashtray?

I first noticed
your missing front
tooth and the way
your body, small,
fragile, trembled

when I hugged
you. I'd whisper,
"You can squeeze
back," and you did.

I thought you'd
never let go.

III

You once asked
about Mother Mary.
I didn't know
how to explain

"virgin." Every word
too large, too
grown for your
young heart.
Vagina.
Penetration.
Rape.
Penis.

And I knew each
would lead to more
questions. I kissed
your forehead, replied,
"an unloved woman."

Your brows crinkled,
heavy in consideration.
"That's me, right?
You asked, "Unloved?"

No. Oh no.

My face tightened
as I spilled,
"I love you, Beckala"
and I wanted,
but couldn't, tell you—
not then, not now—
"Neither of us
are virgins.
Not anymore."

IV

Do you remember
when I filled the bath-
tub cup with luke-
warm water and washed
your white-washed hair?
You said my caramel-
strands reminded you
of silk toffee. I'd shield
your eyes with the edge
of my hand? It seemed
we lived on the edge
of it all, in those simple

lone moments, the only
moments I could protect
you, cover your eyes,
keep you safe
from the sting of soap.

V

Remember how we hid
in Mother's walk-in,
air swollen with stale
moth balls and sweet
lemon oil? We became

something else, someone
else, in that quiet land
of little girls pretending.
Mother's shoes, toes facing
forward, lined along-
side each other
like soldiers prepped

for war. Fake leather.
Embossed patterns
of synthetic snakeskin.
Baby-breath sky
blue. Yellow so creamy
it reminded me of butter.
Crimson dimmed black
in the creases, like

violent bruising.
We both felt bad
for those shoes.
Beckala, you'd choose
flamingo pink, slipping
in your tiny feet,

filling only half.
We stood at attention
and jutted our hips
just like grown-ups

VI

In our after time,
I'd wrap you, Sweet Baby
Sister, curve you
in my arms, wait 'til
your heart slowed
and your eyes slid low.

Then I'd sing.
You'd tell me
my breath reminded
you of buttered corn
and I'd pray my essence
stay and linger with you.

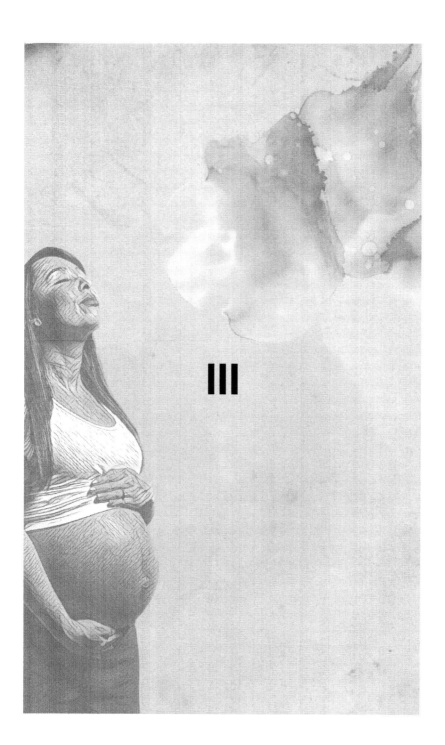

This is not a complete collection of all the tales my body could tell,
but a glimpse, an offering of what my body has done in the world,
what I've done with my body, what has been done to my body.

Seedling

Mother grew me in her womb-room, the only seed
she'd learned to plant, while chain-smoking
her Rothmans king-sized. She sang *She Loves You*
on the train to work, a sheer pink scarf knotted
'round her bottle-redded head. She contrasted
like that. She thought herself a modern girl, blue
jeans rolled below the knees. She thought herself
someone James Dean might find keen. While I grew,
I wondered if she'd any thought of me.

I grew a volunteer lemon tree from a seed the birds
dropped in. I re-planted her near my hammock
where I sway to earth-hums and sing *What's Going On.*
I was born blonde, no, towhead white, and now high-
light my earned-greys. If you ask, I'll admit I'm not
that modern or modest. I drape in wide-legged
trousers that whisk like wind and feel like butter.
I grew that lemon tree, though I never did grow lemons
and somehow, this makes me think of Mother.

My first seed birthed in a patio planter. Purple
Basil. Eagle, Idaho. Circa, 2000. I grew my first
son behind a wall of muscle and sang *How
Great Thou Art,* but only the refrain and off-
key, an octave too low. Later, another son tells
me he remembers growing in my belly. He repeats
this story when he's three or five while curled
into my ribs on his top bunk, the moon
grinning through panes as if hearing my boy's
chatter of those dark-warm-baths-without-toys-
but-better-than-bubbles-and-a-blanket place.

and I wonder why I don't remember
Mother's womb this way.

I build a womb-room beneath the stair-
well and shelve it with books and a night
light that glimmers stars onto the slanted
ceiling. I fill the space with pillows and silk-
woven tosses. I plant myself beneath
the pile. Tell myself I am still seed. I'm still
growing, and, at any moment, I might
sprout, spring forth, like the crocus

breaking through cement.

When her water breaks

She talks to the moon
> tells her her troubles
> a babe on the way
> a pile of unpaid bills
> a worry of wrecking her unborn
> a knowing she's better alone

She won't hide
> her bulging belly, stretching
> muscle and tees and tendons
> her footprints pressed
> in sun-soft tar, crossing neighbor's
> lawns, pathing to her porch

She's arranged
> container gardens
> brimming with basil,
> rosemary, and tomato
> plants that brown and wilt
> despite her watering

Her water breaks
> when she's alone,
> but she's always alone
> except for the babe
> she grows and talks
> to in place of the moon
> because he's closer

She's toweled
> the driver's seat
> as she steers
> herself to delivery
> urging her son
> *stay in, stay put,*
> *wait until we get there*

> unsure she'll ever get there.

Tombstone Roses

My brother introduced me to music and Marilyn's
sticky gloss. At 11, I craved my lips uncrack,

my hips curve wide. My brother knew every
thing, and when he compared me to Marilyn,

I believed. *Oh* how I believed. I'd read about her
upbringing, her neglect (*like me*), her unwanted-

ness (*like me*), and suicidal considerations (*Oh how
I tried. I really tried*). The way she wrestled being

Marilyn. On dates, she'd disappear, (*still like
me*) and later they'd find her staring in a mirror,

asking, *Who am I?* Maybe she would've found her
answer asking other questions—*What am I? Where*

did I go? After I entered the military, I unnamed myself, introduced *Rebecca*, no longer Becky—no

longer victim. Not as drastic as Norma Jean spinning
into Marilyn, though I thought I could alchemy

into gold, story selected memories. My brother
still calls me Becky, but he's the only one. And Tina's

honeyed words—sugared with sweetcorn breath—
singing her name for me (*Beckala*), carries me

to playground swings, high-heel-dress-ups and Daddy's
bad things. I think Norma Jean vanished once she white-

washed into Marilyn. She told Joe, *if I die before
you, leave red roses on my grave each week.*

He promised. *Oh* how he promised. And delivered.
I desire a delivery man, one who brings flowers

to my tombstone, sprinkles petals cross my heart-stone—
keeps his promise, sees me. Sees me better than me.

Kneeling Whispers of Desperate Wants

It begins in prayer and ends on stoned bathroom floors. Wolf turned her to humble-bee, though she'd been warned. Crystalled anger pushed through to surface sweat—that's how silence ruptures. You see her on Can-Ada Road, one street between counties, and you feel no pity: she is home. Her story lives in stones. Your life lived in bottom-line measures. The waters are your friend. Everything washes out. Everything rinses

life. With Divine. Someone said the bark of dog reaches angels. The kneeling whispers of desperate wants reach them too. We will not forget. The bruises on our knees are our becoming. Becoming stone. Where we fell. Brought down by wolf, wise and wanting, stoney star. Not every stone is silent. Neither is every story. Our words pile, like quarries of grief, covering grandmother graves. They meet you to pray.

To petrify. To purify. All baptizing runs: in tears, in sweat, in songs, in lies and loss and love. It sings beneath skin. It tangos on stone, stone shaped with water. Water changes everything—canyons and mountains and mountains and mountains of betrayal. Silence shatters your life, splitting your foundation. We are never far from our ancestors or our knees. The floor is closer than we think.

On a field trip to the Lincoln Park Zoo, a giraffe licked a marshmallow from my hand, its tongue tangled half my arm and for a moment, we connected—beast and beauty—and his spit [which I refused to wipe away] dripped down my elbow. Washing felt like erasure and I wanted the animal to stay with me, offer power. I later learned that silence is a superpower.

I later learned that howling is a mikveh. That immersion can cradle wolf wounds. That mammas would walk across the desert barefoot with babies packed on backs, stepping towards the Promised Land. Their sweat holds story. We pray. We scream. We bark to the heavens. We quit asking for forgiveness. We ask only to be heard.

A Car that Runs Matters

Clocks tick at 3 am. Candles flick-
er as the fridge hums her eternal
earth song. Those small sounds
I miss while traveling through
day, wading through husband-rage.

I sweep bangs from damp
foreheads, kiss cool cheeks
Goodnight, rest my palm
on chests, waiting for whispers
of breath. Their rise. Their

fall. I pray they pardon
my miss-steps. I pad into quiet:
clank locks, click bolts, re-
check doors: closed. Sealed.
Secure. From out-side

intruders. My familiar
round words; *Shhhhh.*
Listen. I love you. I'm
sorry. Forgive me. Thank
you. I fire up my Denali.

Though unable to leave,
I can't manage a dead
battery. My husband,
my master, teaches me
hushed-ways. My closet,

my master, offers space
for my lost voice. My pen
scratches lesions. My body
frees stories. I'll wobble, return to bed, tug sheets, eyes

squeezed in pretend sleep
while I wait for him,
Leave. Then I can rise,
coffee filtering bitter grains
as amber sun bursts sky.

Not the Land of Milk and Honey

Nightfall stretched four miles as the last hummingbird
    took flight into indigo-inked sky
    lone and looking for her scarlet

Petunia. Tubular flowers offer the most
    nectar. And here, in my woven hammock,
    not the land of Milk and Honey, I wake,

my throat dust-dry, a buzzing in my head, worried
    I drank the bottle of Red the night before,
    wondering if the Fighters are flying under

radar. My hummingbird, still flapping, rushes 'round
    like a tiny tornado—73 beats per second—
    as my hammock sways to earth-hum sound.

All I want is sleep and song, more in my body
    than in my brain. Stillness can swallow
    you like a star-less sky, moon

hidden behind mountain, or the other side
    of storm-clouds waiting for the right
    time to thunder. And I wonder

if there's ever a right time—for war or tears
    or feeding a hunger that's selfish
    and red. Wonder if the tubular

felt raped and left for dead after her
    nectar-draining, like blood-drawn
    from empty veins. I want to rise

and toast seeded-bagels, spread them with soft
    cheese and avocados, wash each bite
    with honeyed milk. Let nectar coat

my throat.

Blessed are the PeaceMakers

Blessed are the empty wombs, the wounded and the
lost. The young girls crying in bathwaters. Bless
each boy circumcised later in life and every
sister punished by her brother in the family bed. Bless
sons and daughters who found more honor in unhonoring
every wrong parental
deed.

And bless the babies born breathless and the
red-faced drunkard with his palm stretched in
earnest. Bless

the homemakers, the home-breakers, the ever-present
home-takers. Bless
early frost and late nights and

purple dawns pouring plight,
ending in pimping, bluffing, unblushing—
allowing nothing. Bless the
calloused, the cowards, the less-heard. Bless
eager toddlers longing
Mamma's love
and bless the
kin, the kind, the kindred
ever-after, the after-life, after-birth, the
resurrected. And if no blessings remain,
save the least of us, the last of us, the lone ones stained.

I was once your body shield

(Tina)

Do you remember
when I abandoned
school for marriage?
Beckala, I was 14,
maybe 15, and he,
my first husband,
a military man, held
a hardened jaw
and fisted hands.

I didn't want to desert
you, leave you solo-
flying, fighting Daddy.
That first husband
wouldn't let me bring
you along. It felt like
I left you to die.

I think I did.

Later you searched
the center of your military
life, finding me
in some small Northern
Indiana city. It felt like
you needed to verify
my existence, ensure
someone at sometime
bore some weight
as your human shield.

I thought you'd ask
about Daddy—we
never spoke those words—
not then, not before.

You said I seemed smaller
than you'd remembered.

By then, on my fifth
groom, a fifth Beater,
I'd borne five children
to call my own. You asked
how I kept my sweetness.
Said I still spoke softly.

I couldn't tell you
I rarely said a word,
wouldn't tell you
how rarely I'd been

heard. When we hugged, you felt
all bones and I knew starvation
as your way to disappear, to live
un-noticed by men, remain
untouched, unharmed.

You told me buttered
corn lived as one of few
starches you allowed
because it reminded you
of me. And I held you—you—

now taller than me, now
smaller than me, and I cried
the guilt cry of a mother
who orphaned her baby,
only to have her
return fractured.
You held your tears
like a tight cocoon.
I saw your lips move,
something like chanting,
something like prayer.

Steroids cannot cure hunger

1. when tight, the iliotibial band creates friction
2. pelvic to shin—with knee between—pains and pulls
3. pain: a symptom something's wrong
4. runners often experience IT band syndrome
5. new mothers sitting crisscross while breastfeeding endure ITB syndrome too
6. an unlatched preemie proves deadly
7. an unlatched front door feels perilous as well
8. one new baby survived six days abandoned in a dumpster
9. the houseless survive on dumpster waste every day
10. you can fix ITB syndrome with ice, rest, and steroid shots
11. pain: a symptom something's not right
12. ice and rest and steroids cannot cure hunger
13. you cannot force a baby to latch if he-she-they lack hunger
14. unpain: avoid activities that trigger pain
15. how can you avoid the pang of empty arms and womb?
16. it's impossible to ice your own heart

On the Road to Tarring Tender Bellies

My tire spun before me. No. Untrue. Rubber chunks splatted my windscreen.
Certain a bird shat an innertube or a lifeboat. Certain a phoenix flew in for
a rescue, for our escape. I swerved—to the edge, to embankment—rattled
and stopped. My sons, still and asleep, silent the same way

I'd stayed silent in the center of my road. Certain sky would break
and winged angels would backpack me up and out of the driver's seat.
Later, I'll learn to fly that way, stretch my legs long, let loose, and cruise
where the wind willed. Become my own phoenix.

I packed my babies into pockets, onto breasts, fire-walking asphalt instead.
My feet tarred, my feathers fallen—my tender underbelly exposed.
I'll wag my arms, babies latched, wind pulsing beneath my lift.
Certain we'll steer near the sun. Certain we'll melt

into one.

Life Lines

⌄‾⌄‾⌄‾‾

Monitors stream, like river maps linking fragile beats.

⌄‾⌄‾⌄‾

Hold this single life-tone, heart-song—

⌄‾⌄‾⌄‾

wait—watch. Note vague, invisible rise.

⌄‾⌄‾⌄‾

Note fall. Note his struggle, wrestling one breath.

⌄‾⌄‾⌄‾

He needs: a pacemaker to pace him, intervention to simply

⌄‾⌄‾⌄‾

I need a drink and a smoke and something hard, something
sleep.

⌄‾⌄‾⌄‾

When sun breaks horizon, shattering line between sky and dirt, I'll sway
with the soundless tone of morning, songless hum.

‾‾‾‾‾

Batman Doesn't Pack a Piece

In the middle of a line
— *an offering*—
my son reminds me,
"You promised
to play Mario Party."

Reminds me,
"You're a woman
of your word."

I'm built of words
—*my body in the world.*

The line beckons me
—*what's been done*
to my body—
pulls me to my page.

Interruption.
—*all the tales*
my body could tell.
He knocks with hesitation.

I find my journal,
jot my line:
—*a glimpse of what*
I've done
with my body,
what's been done
to my body—

say it aloud,
hoping to keep
my thread,
remember
where to head.

He forgets
to show me
which button
helps my princess
—*my body knows*—
helps her roll.

I laugh.
He squints his eyes
to half-moons, tosses
his head and banters
the way only boys do.

My princess rushes
through fruit
— *a complete collection*
of bodytales—
and I'm in his world,
his place of make-
believe, where any-
thing can happen
and most things go
right instead of wrong.

My line—*my body.*

Earlier, the neighbor-
hood boys gathered
on the lawn, nerf-
gun-armed
—*done with my body.*

They donned
costumes
from garage bins
— *done to my body.*

Luke fought alongside
Captain America
while Batman loaded
an assault rifle.

My line—*my body.*

I remind my boy:
Batman doesn't
pack a piece.

He reminds me,
"This is pretend."

I remember:
my chores, groceries,
and to-dos. I worry
over unpaid bills,
pressing controller
buttons, moving
my princess
in and out of obstacles,
in and out of trouble.

He snaps me from my trance.

I've lost:
my line,
my thought,
my art
—*this is not complete*—

Forgot:
I'm a writer.
A mother.

No.

I'm a princess.
I gather star-points.
I leap strawberries.
I run to the finish line.

Fused

My heart hides, she builds pop-up tents, climbs inside.
She runs slow, stays low, fifty-five flutters a minute.

My son's heart arrives damaged—fused valves.
Half-open. Half-shut. His beating sound resounds

drummers in cartoon jingles—*Scooby Scooby-Doo,*
Where Are You? He tips the scales at 20 grams,

flickers like a fairy fly who houses the least
heart of all living creatures. His host, my son,

four pounds at birth, weighed larger in my palms,
larger in my memory. My heart knows

a broken heart as a medical syndrome, flushing hormones
into her host's system. Her clutching smacks of heart

attacks, though she's not a violent organ. My boy's
heart strums, flapping his aortic cusps, his seals

seeping while I'm dreaming he suffers little. I pray
for zero backflow, worry his rush will surely flush

his remaining beats. He worries about himself.
Worries he might quit, because he did. Sometimes.

There's such a thing as death from a broken heart,
surely this will be the way my heart goes, the end

of her flow. She's weighty, wanting to touch her own pulse,
her whooshed vibration. She believes she's useful

to her body-house, that she'll sprout wings—not
for flight—but for howl, for pollinating the world in blood.

My boy's heart trembles his tiny dance, turns my son
ashen, tired, and aged. When I wake, I fear he's surrendered,

the bed imprinted with the shape of my son.

Lost in the Dryer Vent

I measure minutes in sips of chai, honey-fused, steamy, creamy, angry, and lost with that Lego brick—the one that held the structure—the one that mattered most—that we'll find later in the dryer vent. I wake from naps more tired, throat dried with the snore that startles my eyes wide. I de-clutter junk drawers but leave stacks of books which turn to furniture—end tables and foot stools and bathtub trays—most marked half-through with feathers and Post-its. I wear fuzzy socks in July heat, but walk barefoot in dewed grass, in rain, in snow. My A-positive blood seems a negative factor and I no longer fight infection, now a life-battle, like the hundred-year war. The body wears, is worn, torn from an era of neglect and hurt. Scar tissue builds and binds us tighter and we lose our range of motion, we lose our range, our sightings down the barrels of assault rifles though we know the burden after assault, we'll wonder, *Where did the honey go?* Perhaps sweetness left when the last bee could no longer reach the stem, make it to the petal's center, lost and startled and stacked, now part of the furniture.

Mostly Garlic and Cilantro I

I quit smoking, I started chocolate. I quit hot sauce, but added Tiger Balm to my neck at night. I quit weighing myself and purchased a scale for the puppy litter and another to measure my anxiety. I quit counting calories and carbs. I counted the number of friends still circling once I turned wilty and wise. I quit turning over a new leaf and decided old leaves can be ironed between waxed sheets along with shaven bits of crayons, preserving autumnal beauty. I never quit coloring, but I quit shadowing my lids. I kept my Reds of Worth satin lipstick. I wore it while I wrote, believing my words improved with a respected Loreal glossed across my mouth. I kept my bamboo sheets, aloe socks, my hot tub beneath the Idaho star-dripping sky. I wanted to smoke because I wanted a habit that felt normal, wanted the taste of something other than bile on my tongue. I quit swiping my pits with aluminum-ladened deodorant. I started noticing my aroma, mostly garlic and cilantro, not unpleasant, but who wants to smell like a main course first thing? I quit consuming chemicals—through my skin, within my food, in the news. I started collecting volunteer marigolds, re-birthing them near companion plants so maybe a community could be cultured; one that deters aphids and slugs. Okay. I never was a smoker, not a real one, but I tried. One time, under the influence of Angel Envy, I smoked someone else's pack, flicked the ashes on a fake gas flame. I framed my beds with sprouted garlic and enticed predators—praying mantises and ladybugs—to prey on the unintimidated creatures. I invited the pollinators—the Honeys, The Bumbles, The Hummingbirds—and purposefully deposited milkweeds, seducing the Monarchs. I kept my hair long, told myself I looked either a mermaid or a crone. I kept my wardrobe and color-coded methods – organizing scarves and the tone of poetry and spices and, yes, sometimes men. I embraced mid-fifty invisibility. There's magic in remaining unseen and resentment once you understand you're unheard or silenced or worse. Though, what's worse? I quit praying for myself and started kneeling for the dead, the departed, the broken-hearted. I spilled my ink on square pages and gave spare change to tzedakah and lit extra candles and incensed cinnamon with sage and cloves. I added cloves to coffee. I added more honey to bagels and oatmeal and chai and bruises and scabs and marigold petals. I quit trying to smoke.

A King for Me

The first night I slept
kid-less, I scattered side-
ways, crisscross my
mattress, moving without
worry I'd stir my sons

awake. I never dreamed
my boy could love
a girl, hand her his hoodies
& unlace my embrace.
I never pictured my son

singing *You Shook Me
All Night Long,* asking
me, *Stop*, when I sing along,
just us traveling: me, riding
shotgun. Him, steering

through unlit Idaho back-
roads with one headlight
and a loose bumper.
I was less prepped
for his, *Were you wild*

at my age? I shrugged:
not quite an answer,
not quite a lie. I wanted
him to believe the best
of me. Later, he'll crash

my car, I'll say, *It's okay,*
adding, *We all crash at
times.* I'm certain he
speeds when I'm not there.
Certain he curses his lack

of father-care. He grew
quick—ripping tendons,
stretching knees. He
swelled into goodness,
into kindness, and unlike

the men who came before,
he's teaching his disabled
brother, teaching him to fry
an egg, shave, and shift
go-kart gears. Tells him, *Wear
protective gear.*

He nestles in that full-boy,
full-body way, pauses
his game, his girl, to change
      a light bulb,
           a tire,

                  my view

                      of men.

The Wildlife Protection Plan

I tossed a rock
with my son.
It broke through
the face of shallow lake,
sinking, hide & seeking

behind bold cattails,
breathing stark rays.
Someone once

told me submerging
could cleanse me,
offer new starts,
if only I believed.

(And. Oh! I did.
I believed.)

Water never worked
that way for me. It rinsed
me out, washed me
over, eroded bone

and breath, one ripple
pulsing into two, then
three, then many. Waves
crashing, swelling my belly.

Wanna skip those stones? my boy asks.

(I do. Oh! I really do.)

I don't know how
to skip—anything.
Certain I'll scatter
like pebbles lining
the ocean floor.

A mottled Mallard
paddles through, her brown-
speckled plumage breaking
mirrored surface, her
babies tugging to keep
her steady pace.
Wait, my son grips my wrist.
We don't want to hurt her.

No, I say and mean it.
(Oh! How I mean it.)

The Non-Standard Parenting Plan
for Turning Boys into Men

- ❏ Before you show, before you even know, take Folic Acid. Rest.
- ❏ Read *What to Expect When You're Expecting.*
- ❏ Worry.
- ❏ Unlearn normal baby-care. Preemies are special breeds.
- ❏ Listen for breath.
- ❏ Live on little sleep.
- ❏ Hold him—heart against heart.
- ❏ Sync yourself.
- ❏ Forget self-feeding. Or showering. Or writing.
- ❏ Wonder: is it abuse if your husband bashes? Your arm?
- ❏ Tell yourself, *So long as he doesn't harm the children.*
- ❏ Teach your sons to pee standing, aiming for Fruit Loops in the toilet.
- ❏ Redefine *Harm.*
- ❏ Take the Victim Protection Counsellor's advice: pack a duffle for each son.
- ❏ Bundle medical supplies, birth certificates, the breast pump.
- ❏ Escape.
- ❏ Seek shelter in a safe house.
- ❏ Food, shelter, safety. Basic needs turn scarce.
- ❏ Find a way.
- ❏ Find your military training pays, push-ups work for re-direction.
- ❏ Stretch a loaf of bread an entire week. Build hamburgers from rice and beans.
- ❏ Rebuild yourself.
- ❏ Answer honestly. If they're old enough to ask, they're old enough to know truth.
- ❏ Titanium and bone-graft your fractured neck. Seal your fractured heart. Show your sons you're not a survivor, you're an overcomer. [While you're at it, show yourself.]
- ❏ Build blanket forts. Brew cleaning potions. Grow fruit trees from discarded seeds.
- ❏ Read stories by flashlight late at night.
- ❏ Recycle. Repurpose.
- ❏ Learn to cook with flour, water, salt, and sugar. Bake challah, bagels, cinnamon incense.
- ❏ Write poetry on scrolls. Tie them on trees.

- [ ] Fill a free little library.
- [ ] Pray for the sick, the weary, the hungry, yourself.
- [ ] Attend grad school. Twice.
- [ ] Train them how to date, to ask permission, to chew with their mouths closed.
- [ ] Show them how to: press deodorant through body hair, shave beards, hold doors for strangers.
- [ ] Tell them to value their own body and the bodies of others.
- [ ] Treat your car as parental training ground. Bring bananas and condoms and demonstrate safe sex at stop lights.
- [ ] Sing aloud in public when they misbehave. Get the lyrics wrong.
- [ ] Dance to AC/DC in front of their peers.
- [ ] Say *I'm sorry*. Say it often.
- [ ] Gift them private journals where they can ask you anything.
- [ ] Promise to keep their secrets.
- [ ] Keep every promise.
- [ ] Heal through written word, tear-stained pillows, house-saging rituals.
- [ ] Teach them forgiveness.
- [ ] Offer yourself as the scapegoat—they may call you any time, any day, any hour.
- [ ] Permit them to call you a crazy Jewish mom. Behave accordingly.
- [ ] Remind them life is temporary and they are souls journeying in bags of skin.
- [ ] Tell them *Thank you* for choosing you.
- [ ] Remind them their ancestors would be proud.
- [ ] Remember not to lose yourself along the way.

Meat & Dairy

I roam my home and sit with ghosts—one ghost in particular. I roam with my perfect-man ghost and think this is why dating proves complicated. I'm thinking no man competes with perfect-men-ghosts. I'll roam and think and sip my tea, infuse it with honey and cloves. I'll sip and think that someday my flesh-man might meet my ghost-man and my worlds might just collide.

I eat meat on one dish, dairy on another and the two of them are never together. Dairy and meat are not to meet. I wash dishes in separate sinks. A dairy sink. A meat sink. I consider my bathroom sinks meat since I am flesh stretched 'cross bone and filament. I eat alone, chew slow, dip my tongue in honey and cloves. I consider honeying my pressed lips, keeping my lips together, keeping myself together while keeping—my ghost and my man, my meat and my dairy—apart.

I sit still, restrict the urge to touch myself, knowing it's only steam-release, knowing if I self-touch, I'll sit with more loneliness, even if my ghost is near. I still sit. I restrict. My ghost unable to touch me. Stillness turns me edgy and those tiny mishaps, like a dirty dish in the wrong sink, steams me. I sit, restricting and steaming—all necessary disciplines. I'll redirect *that* cloved energy. I'll alchemy, channel into something surprising, something that turns my head.

In stillness, I dream of butter-slathered bagels, chunking pieces onto my tongue. I'll sing for that sting of salt and sesames crusting my honeyed lips. The kettle sings while she steams and I brew a chai with cloved honey and dollop one controlled spoonful of cream. My control pays well. I tell myself to brew a mental buffet. While still, I'll turn to Limon, Laux, Dubrow. I'll lose myself in words and turn dog-eared pages. Lose myself so I don't lose myself.

I control myself in weighted dreams. Weights draped 'cross me. 60 pounds holding me down, holding me so I don't roam too soon, though my ghost coaxes me towards sky. I soar in my dreams, control my body in night-flight, restricting space and time. I still time. I move space. I move nearer Light—re-fill, re-fuel, prepare for tomorrow. If there be a tomorrow. And if there be a tomorrow, I'm prepared.

Tomorrow, I'll sip and eat and forget my preparedness as the sun cascades 'round earth and my body-pain sinks through. Despite my ghost-mate, loneliness drapes, cloving and crusting my dreams. I'll forget I'm a spiritual creature trapped in body, draped in skin. I'll forget I've filled myself the night before, forget until my flesh-son hugs me, his skin steaming of meat and dairy and boy-dirt. His scent stills me in that one particular second, and in that second, my ghost departs, and I am lone and lost until I remember. I remember. I'm still. I'm here. I'm still here.

Mostly Garlic and Cilantro II

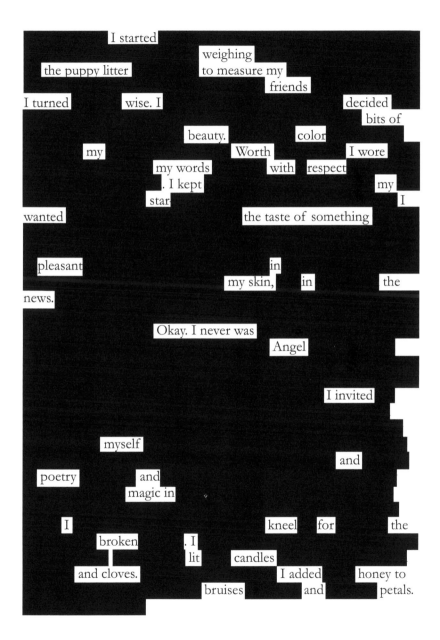

I started
weighing
the puppy litter   to measure my
friends
I turned   wise. I   decided
bits of
beauty.   color
my   Worth   I wore
my words   with   respect
. I kept   my
star   I
wanted   the taste of something

pleasant   in
my skin,   in   the
news.

Okay. I never was

Angel

I invited

myself

and

poetry   and
magic in

I   kneel   for   the
broken   . I
lit   candles
and cloves.   I added   honey to
bruises   and   petals.

Yellow Declaration

After slurping sweet-creamed turmeric tea, my bottom lip stained yellow,
like dandelion heads before whispering to cotton when winds whisk their yellows.

I wait for wars to end & love to begin & at mid-point mid-life, I can't see
the difference between the two. Each old, faded, and unyellowed.

I wait for you, Love. I wait even longer for me, though I wonder if I'll know
myself when I see myself, my hair wiry & gray, no longer bleached yellow.

I ask only to know my sons, maybe by their smell, by their smile.
No. I ask they recognize me still, years after I'm under, my yell low.

I ate. I consumed memory. Ate loss. I ate, though not enough buffets
to fill war wounds & body hate. I binged. I purged. Bile brewed, yellowed.

My journal holds my angst, my blessings. I pen body-story & fairy tale,
tracing veins & scars like road maps—bruised black & honey-yellow.

If my writings prove too hard to read, should they be left unread, by you,
by your mother, by the Father? Should the pages sit, singed & yellowed?

And words that offer disruption & discomfort, aren't they the lines
we should speak? The phrases spit from between our teeth, dark & yellow?

Perhaps the world should weave the unspoken, the unthinkable—
incest, rape—lore of those taken too soon, too old, too yellow.

Shout these with our morning blessings. Preach them from pulpit, from bars.
Kneel as you howl in honor of the girls lost, silenced, & yellowed.

Breakfast became my blessing. Bagel toasted, stained with unsalted butter, & a single
perfectly poached egg, its belly soft & slightly peppered. The yolk, deep yellow.

My yard grows volunteers, sunflowers pregnant with seeds, milkweed, Russian
olives & orange poppies, along with one lemon tree, fruit sour & yellow.

All my hair is blonde or white or stress-strung & curled. Eyelashes. Eyebrows. Arm hair so light it offers sheen when I'm tan. Even my pubes are gold or gray or yellow.

Some say detasseling corn is like rape, savaging female stalk centers. But I, Rebecca, declare, don't compare rape to anything but rape or yellow

to anything but yellow.

At the end of my shrinking

In the end was the endless buffet and the buffet was crowded
in the end I was crowded in the end I was empty &
small holding my child-stories when I wore Garanimals & later
I turned to fashion   crowded my closet   crowded my drawers
crowded my mind & my time & my planner & my dinner plate
I went back for thirds   & fifths   more than the other
larger diners   I stayed small   grew smaller &
breastless & amenorrheic purging every morsel up & out

I grew   up   and I knew   that I was too small   too silent
with the boys because I was taught so well by the Father who crowded
my bed at night, crowded each crevice with his man-ness, crowded
my heart in cloud and storm

I knew   the difficulty of loving   mostly myself   & so I
shrank and shrank and shrank   like those Shrinky Dinks you bake
in the oven until they turn hard and half their size I tornadoed
through that oven door   wore the latest trousers   packed
the popular tote used fashion to hide   my thinness
used fashion to hide
      and that was the end   the end of crowds & buffets &
perfectly matched Garanimal outfits selected by some adult who thought
color-coding clothes a good idea but it prevented the child from
choice & selection   from her own style   &   voice
      and that was the end   I am not my dinner plate
or the size beneath draped dungarees or form-fitting gowns or spandex
now at the end   at the end of my shrinking

I am a buffet   I am the latest fashion   I am my child-
story   I am thinness & thickness   I am Grrrrr – Animal
I   am

I wanted you to know
(Rebecca)

I remember. Oh! I remember
the way we thrashed into woman-
hood, though still girls,
and my unhappiness over
my breast-less-ness—always
less noticed—and you,
you were not so lucky.

Oh Tina! I remember
we grew more motherless
each passing day, bearing
witness to our taken innocence
as he powered over us, on top
of us, our petals dropping

to stone, crushed under-
foot. *Oh, I remember!*
Sunday morning sky
as you dabbed my lips pink,
painting me bright and pushed
my cheeks into smile. You told
me I was Beautiful. Beautiful.

Remember?

And that time we sipped tea
with teddy bears and you
said we weren't *that*
special, said there's another
sister somewhere, her fist
stifling cries. A sister,
somewhere, going down,
going under. And later:

Too many sisters.
Not enough sisters.

Later, I'll remember and plant
poppies for you on a meadow
in England, in my backyard,
in my heart. They'll burst pods
to dirt, face clouds and, despite
rain, they'll keep growing,
keep going.

I'll remember you in my dreams—
your fawn eyes and buttered-
corn breath—my body tossing,
grieving your cost to keep me
safe. Though, you never could
keep me safe, you kept me
contained in our bruised
exit wound, kept me warm
in our after time.

Every time. *Oh!*
How I remember.

Remember?

Acknowledgements

A mug of steamy, honeyed chai to my mentors and teachers, some who worked directly with me, others whose books I've valued and studied. I still do. A special thanks to Gayle Brandeis, Brian Turner, Lee Herrick, Ken Rodgers, Steven Church, Suzanne Roberts, and Patricia Smith—all who pushed me through essaying and into poetic language, into a place I could access some of my most difficult and inaccessible stories, those trapped, boxed in my body.

I'm grateful to all the editors from publications where many of these poems initially appeared, often in various forms:

The Limberlost Review, Hypertext Magazine, Survivor Lit, The Elpis Pages, The Poetic Bond X, and *Paragraph Literary Journal.*

And I'm filled with gratitude for the MFA Creative Writing Program at the University of Nevada, Reno at Lake Tahoe; The Poetry Foundation; SunJune; Yetzirah Poets; PITCOT; Betty Rodgers; Roberts' Rejection Club; The Accountability Club; my BSU students; My juvie participants, and the International Women's Writing Guild. A very special thanks to my first reader of all things I write, Lorene, who has stuck with my early drafts for over 20 years. It is within community and camaraderie that I am developed and shaped into artist.

Thank you, Moon Tide Press, for believing in me.

Thank you to Zachary, Preston, and Julian. Without you, there'd be little of me in the world.

Notes

"Honor Thy Mother" is a rotating anaphoric poem and a golden shovel after "Unspoken."

"Of Birth and Blessings" is a rotating anaphoric poem and a golden shovel after "A Soft Food Diet Doesn't Always Heal the Heart."

Though unusual for an artist to create a golden shovel after his/her/their own work, *Tangled by Blood* presents poems in conversation with one another, offering a continuance, a lingering, much like violence lingers. Sometimes for generations. Childhood sexual violence is not an easy topic to discuss, but it must be included in our conversations. It must. Too many victims are still silenced. Too many victims carry their untold damage, and it trickles into their lives—in fractured relationships, addictions, self-harm, and more.

Keep the conversation going.

About the Author

Evans is a memoirist, poet, and essayist. In addition to writing, she teaches Creative Nonfiction at Boise State University and mentors high school girls in the juvenile system. In her spare time, she co-hosts a radio program, Writer to Writer, offering a space for writers to offer tips on craft and life. She's also disabled, a Veteran, a Jew, a gardener, a mother, a worrier, and more. She has a passion for sharing difficult stories about vulnerability woven with mysticism.

Evans earned two MFAs, one in creative nonfiction, the other in poetry, University of Nevada, Reno at Lake Tahoe. She lives in Idaho with her sons, her Newfoundlands, and her Calico.

Her poems and essays have appeared in *Narratively, The Rumpus, Entropy Literary Magazine, War, Literature & the Arts, The Limberlost Review*, and a handful of anthologies. She's co-edited an anthology of poems, *When There Are Nine; Poems Clebrating the Life and Achievements of Ruth Bader Ginsburg* (Moon Tide Press).

Also Available from Moon Tide Press

Maze Mouth, Brian Sonia-Wallace (2023)
Another Way of Loving Death, Jeremy Ra (2023)
Kissing the Wound, J.D. Isip (2023)
Feed It to the River, Terhi K. Cherry (2022)
Beat Not Beat: An Anthology of California Poets Screwing on the Beat and Post-Beat Tradition (2022)
When There Are Nine: Poems Celebrating the Life and Achievements of Ruth Bader Ginsburg (2022)
The Knife Thrower's Daughter, Terri Niccum (2022)
2 Revere Place, Aruni Wijesinghe (2022)
Here Go the Knives, Kelsey Bryan-Zwick (2022)
Trumpets in the Sky, Jerry Garcia (2022)
Threnody, Donna Hilbert (2022)
A Burning Lake of Paper Suns, Ellen Webre (2021)
Instructions for an Animal Body, Kelly Gray (2021)
Head *V* Heart: New & Selected Poems, Rob Sturma (2021)
Sh!t Men Say to Me: A Poetry Anthology in Response to Toxic Masculinity (2021)
Flower Grand First, Gustavo Hernandez (2021)
Everything is Radiant Between the Hates, Rich Ferguson (2020)
When the Pain Starts: Poetry as Sequential Art, Alan Passman (2020)
This Place Could Be Haunted If I Didn't Believe in Love, Lincoln McElwee (2020)
Impossible Thirst, Kathryn de Lancellotti (2020)
Lullabies for End Times, Jennifer Bradpiece (2020)
Crabgrass World, Robin Axworthy (2020)
Contortionist Tongue, Dania Ayah Alkhouli (2020)
The only thing that makes sense is to grow, Scott Ferry (2020)
Dead Letter Box, Terri Niccum (2019)
Tea and Subtitles: Selected Poems 1999-2019, Michael Miller (2019)
At the Table of the Unknown, Alexandra Umlas (2019)
The Book of Rabbits, Vince Trimboli (2019)
Everything I Write Is a Love Song to the World, David McIntire (2019)
Letters to the Leader, HanaLena Fennel (2019)
Darwin's Garden, Lee Rossi (2019)
Dark Ink: A Poetry Anthology Inspired by Horror (2018)
Drop and Dazzle, Peggy Dobreer (2018)
Junkie Wife, Alexis Rhone Fancher (2018)

The Moon, My Lover, My Mother, & the Dog, Daniel McGinn (2018)
Lullaby of Teeth: An Anthology of Southern California Poetry (2017)
Angels in Seven, Michael Miller (2016)
A Likely Story, Robbi Nester (2014)
Embers on the Stairs, Ruth Bavetta (2014)
The Green of Sunset, John Brantingham (2013)
The Savagery of Bone, Timothy Matthew Perez (2013)
The Silence of Doorways, Sharon Venezio (2013)
Cosmos: An Anthology of Southern California Poetry (2012)
Straws and Shadows, Irena Praitis (2012)
In the Lake of Your Bones, Peggy Dobreer (2012)
I Was Building Up to Something, Susan Davis (2011)
Hopeless Cases, Michael Kramer (2011)
One World, Gail Newman (2011)
What We Ache For, Eric Morago (2010)
Now and Then, Lee Mallory (2009)
Pop Art: An Anthology of Southern California Poetry (2009)
In the Heaven of Never Before, Carine Topal (2008)
A Wild Region, Kate Buckley (2008)
Carving in Bone: An Anthology of Orange County Poetry (2007)
Kindness from a Dark God, Ben Trigg (2007)
A Thin Strand of Lights, Ricki Mandeville (2006)
Sleepyhead Assassins, Mindy Nettifee (2006)
Tide Pools: An Anthology of Orange County Poetry (2006)
Lost American Nights: Lyrics & Poems, Michael Ubaldini (2006)

Patrons

Moon Tide Press would like to thank the following people for their support in helping publish the finest poetry from the Southern California region. To sign up as a patron, visit www.moontidepress.com or send an email to publisher@moontidepress.com.

Anonymous
Robin Axworthy
Conner Brenner
Nicole Connolly
Bill Cushing
Susan Davis
Kristen Baum DeBeasi
Peggy Dobreer
Kate Gale
Dennis Gowans
Alexis Rhone Fancher
HanaLena Fennel
Half Off Books & Brad T. Cox
Donna Hilbert
Jim & Vicky Hoggatt
Michael Kramer
Ron Koertge & Bianca Richards
Gary Jacobelly
Ray & Christi Lacoste
Jeffery Lewis
Zachary & Tammy Locklin
Lincoln McElwee
David McIntire
José Enrique Medina
Michael Miller & Rachanee Srisavasdi
Michelle & Robert Miller
Ronny & Richard Morago
Terri Niccum
Andrew November
Jeremy Ra
Luke & Mia Salazar
Jennifer Smith
Roger Sponder
Andrew Turner
Rex Wilder
Mariano Zaro
Wes Bryan Zwick